ALL AROUND THE WORLD
NETHERLANDS

by Kristine Spanier, MLIS

pogo

Ideas for Parents and Teachers

Pogo Books let children practice reading informational text while introducing them to nonfiction features such as headings, labels, sidebars, maps, and diagrams, as well as a table of contents, glossary, and index.

Carefully leveled text with a strong photo match offers early fluent readers the support they need to succeed.

Before Reading

• "Walk" through the book and point out the various nonfiction features. Ask the student what purpose each feature serves.

• Look at the glossary together. Read and discuss the words.

Read the Book

• Have the child read the book independently.

• Invite him or her to list questions that arise from reading.

After Reading

• Discuss the child's questions. Talk about how he or she might find answers to those questions.

• Prompt the child to think more. Ask: Many dairy farms are in the Netherlands. Do you live near farms? What do they produce?

Pogo Books are published by Jump!
5357 Penn Avenue South
Minneapolis, MN 55419
www.jumplibrary.com

Library of Congress Cataloging-in-Publication Data

Names: Spanier, Kristine, author.
Title: Netherlands / by Kristine Spanier.
Description: Minneapolis, MN: Jump!, [2021]
Series: All around the world | Includes index.
Audience: Ages 7-10 | Audience: Grades 2-3
Identifiers: LCCN 2019045674 (print)
LCCN 2019045675 (ebook)
ISBN 9781645273448 (hardcover)
ISBN 9781645273455 (paperback)
ISBN 9781645273462 (ebook)
Subjects: LCSH: Netherlands–Juvenile literature.
Classification: LCC DJ18 .S68 2021 (print)
LCC DJ18 (ebook) | DDC 949.2–dc23
LC record available at https://lccn.loc.gov/2019045674
LC ebook record available at https://lccn.loc.gov/2019045675

Editor: Jenna Gleisner
Designer: Molly Ballanger

Photo Credits: JacobH/iStock, cover, 5; RamonaS/Shutterstock, 1; Pixfiction/Shutterstock, 3; Vladislav Zolotov/iStock, 4; David Peperkamp/iStock, 6-7; gianliguuori/iStock, 8-9; Sanit Fuangnakhon/Shutterstock, 10; fokke baarssen/Shutterstock, 11; Opla/iStock, 12-13; Frans Sellies/Getty, 14-15; Natali Zakharova/Shutterstock, 16l; sara_winter/iStock, 16r; S-F/Shutterstock, 17; Ingram Publishing/SuperStock, 18-19; RobertHoetink/iStock, 20-21; Oliver Hoffmann/Shutterstock, 21; RomanR/Shutterstock, 23.

Printed in the United States of America at Corporate Graphics in North Mankato, Minnesota.

TABLE OF CONTENTS

CHAPTER 1

WELCOME TO THE NETHERLANDS!

Would you like to visit De Haar Castle? This is the largest castle in the Netherlands! Welcome!

De Haar Castle

Visit a tulip field. Or go to a tulip festival! Tulips are everywhere here. You can also see **windmills**.

windmill

tulips

Amsterdam is the **capital**. It is the home of the Royal Palace. The king or queen is crowned here.

The government meets in The Hague. A **prime minister** is the head of the government.

DID YOU KNOW?

Some Caribbean islands are part of this **kingdom**. The largest are Aruba, Saint Martin, and Curaçao.

Royal
Palace

cheese market

cheese

Dairy farms in the Netherlands produce milk, butter, and many kinds of cheeses. The town of Edam is known for its cheese. People buy it at the cheese market.

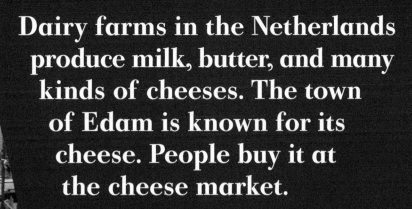

CHAPTER 2

WATER, WATER EVERYWHERE

Netherlands means "low-lying country." Many parts of this country are below **sea level**. Windmills were once used to pump water from land back into the sea.

canal

Many areas have **canals**.
People travel on them.
They take boats from
place to place.

Rotterdam

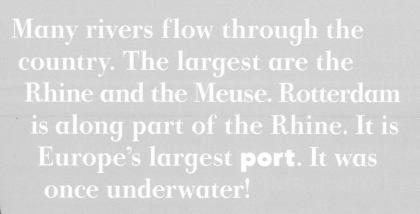

Many rivers flow through the country. The largest are the Rhine and the Meuse. Rotterdam is along part of the Rhine. It is Europe's largest **port**. It was once underwater!

WHAT DO YOU THINK?

People here have learned how to control water. Does nature make life challenging where you live? How so? How have people adjusted to it?

Lake Beemster was drained in 1612. Beemster **Polder** was created. Canals and **dikes** keep water contained. This created space for homes and farmland.

Beemster Polder

TAKE A LOOK!

The Dutch developed different ways to control water. What were some of them?

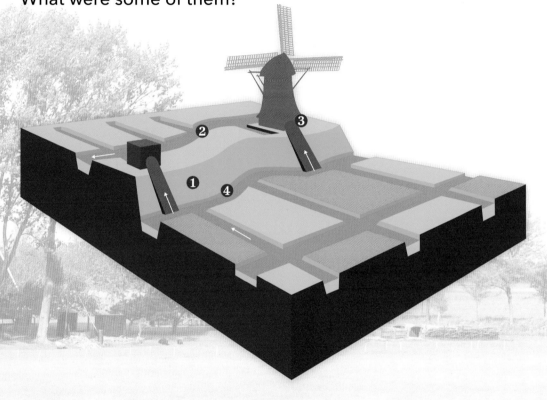

① **dike:** a high wall that is built to hold back water and prevent flooding
② **canal:** a channel dug for water to travel in
③ **windmill:** a structure that pumps water out of lowlands and back to rivers
④ **ditch:** a narrow trench that drains water away

CHAPTER 3

PEOPLE OF THE NETHERLANDS

Would you like to try a stroopwafel? This is a wafer filled with a caramel syrup. Pannekoeken are rolled-up pancakes. You can put your favorite ingredients inside!

stroopwafel

pannekoeken

There are more bikes than people here! Bike paths are all over the country. Why? They keep bikers safe. Amsterdam has a parking ramp just for bikes. It can hold thousands of bikes!

bike parking ramp

Children here start school when they are five years old. Most go until they are 18. Students learn English in grade school.

High school students go to school for two years. Then they have a choice. They can spend the next two years preparing for college. Or they spend those two years preparing for a job.

St. Nicholas

St. Nicholas Eve is celebrated on December 5. Children receive gifts in their shoes! Speculaas cookies are a special treat for the holiday. They have fun designs on them.

Christmas and Easter are important holidays here, too. Would you like to visit?

speculaas

QUICK FACTS & TOOLS

AT A GLANCE

NETHERLANDS

Location: northwestern Europe

Size: 16,040 square miles (41,543 square kilometers)

Population: 17,151,228 (July 2018 estimate)

Capital: Amsterdam

Type of Government: parliamentary constitutional monarchy

Languages: Dutch, Frisian, English

Exports: chemicals, livestock, machinery and transport equipment

Currency: euro

GLOSSARY

canals: Water-filled channels that are dug across land so that boats can travel between two bodies of water.

capital: A city where government leaders meet.

dikes: High walls or dams that are built to hold back water and prevent flooding.

kingdom: An area that is ruled by a king or a queen.

polder: A piece of low-lying land that has been made available for human use by changing natural conditions, such as the flow of water by use of dikes and canals.

port: A town with a harbor where ships can load and unload goods.

prime minister: The leader of a country.

provinces: Districts or regions in a country.

sea level: The average level of the ocean's surface, used as a starting point from which to measure the height or depth of a place.

windmills: Structures with long blades that turn in the wind and produce power that is used to pump water, grind grain into flour, or generate electricity.

Netherlands currency

INDEX

TO LEARN MORE

Finding more information is as easy as 1, 2, 3.

1. Go to www.factsurfer.com
2. Enter "Netherlands" into the search box.
3. Click the "Surf" button to see a list of websites.

FACT SURFER